WILDLIFE AT RISK

BEARS

Malcolm Penny

Wayland

WILDLIFE AT RISK

Bears
Birds of Prey
Elephants
Gorillas
Tigers
Whales and Dolphins

Series editor: Sue Hadden
Series designer: Marilyn Clay

Cover: An Alaskan brown bear hunting for fish.

First published in 1990 by
Wayland (Publishers) Ltd
61 Western Road, Hove
East Sussex BN3 1JD

British Library Cataloguing in Publication Data
Penny, Malcolm
  Bears.
  1. Bears
  I. Title II. Series
  599.74446

  ISBN 1–85210–962–9

Typeset by Nicola Taylor, Wayland.
Printed and bound in Italy by LEGO SpA.

Contents

All words printed in **bold** are explained
in the glossary on page 30.

THE FAMILY OF BEARS

Bears are mammals – animals with furry coats and warm blood, which feed their babies with milk. They have sturdy bodies, with short but very strong legs. Most bears' feet are furry underneath and they all have very long claws. Bears have large heads, with small eyes and little rounded ears. Their tails are very short. All bears walk on the soles of their feet, not on their toes like most other mammals.

There are seven main kinds of bear. We call each kind a **species**. The biggest is the polar bear, which lives in the icy Arctic. The brown bear and the American black bear are also very large. The smallest bear is the sun bear from Malaysia. The map below shows where they all live.

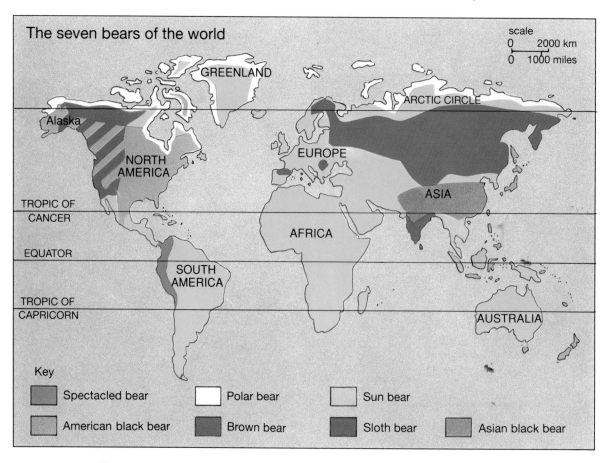

The seven bears of the world

scale
0   2000 km
0   1000 miles

GREENLAND

ARCTIC CIRCLE

Alaska

NORTH AMERICA

EUROPE

ASIA

TROPIC OF CANCER

AFRICA

EQUATOR

SOUTH AMERICA

TROPIC OF CAPRICORN

AUSTRALIA

Key

Spectacled bear | Polar bear | Sun bear

American black bear | Brown bear | Sloth bear | Asian black bear

All bears, except one, can climb well, and most of them eat only plants. The polar bear is different: it does not need to climb, because it lives where there are no trees, and it eats meat. Bears do not have very good eyesight or hearing but they have an excellent sense of smell.

Left *The small sun bear is in danger because its forest habitat is being cut down.*

The fur under a polar bear's feet helps it to walk on slippery ice.

HOW BEARS LIVE

Bears are large animals and they need plenty of space in which to find their food. They are not often found in large groups. Usually a family is made up of a mother and her cubs. The males live alone for most of the year, except during the **breeding season**.

Male and female sun bears and sloth bears stay together for their whole life. With the other species of bears, the males **mate** with any female in their **territory** who is ready to mate with them.

Female bears defend a smaller territory of their own.

A grizzly bear cub waits for its mother to catch a salmon from a bubbling Alaskan stream.

They roam about inside it, looking for food and places to rest, for themselves and their **cubs**. Although bears are large and strong, they are peaceful animals. If two families happen to meet, they do not usually fight. They smell each other from quite a long distance, and move out of each other's way.

Having plenty of food is very important, especially during the autumn. This is the time of year when every bear must eat as much as it can, to be as fat as possible when winter comes.

Above *This American black bear has enjoyed a meal from a dead mule deer.*

Left *Young polar bears love to wrestle playfully. As adults, they may need to be able to fight.*

Bears have their young at different times of year, depending on where they live. In the **tropics**, they can breed at any time of year. In places which have a winter, such as the Arctic, Europe and North America, the young are born during the coldest part of the year. The new-born bears are too small to keep warm on their own. However, they are born in a cosy underground hole called a den. They stay there, keeping warm with their mother until spring comes.

This habit of sleeping in the winter is called hibernation. Many different animals do this because they cannot find food during the winter.

This sun bear cub was born at a zoo in Florida, USA.

Their bodies cool down and their hearts beat very slowly, so that they use up the fat in their bodies as slowly as possible.

Bears do not hibernate, even though they stay in their dens through the winter. They remain just as warm as usual, and their hearts beat at the usual speed. This is why their autumn feast is so important. They must have an enormous store of fat to keep them alive until they can come out again in spring to look for food.

Right *A black bear in its den.*

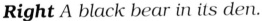

Left *A seven-month old grizzly bear cub ventures out in spring. It will not stray far from its mother.*

BEARS IN THE HUMAN WORLD

Bears need a lot of space and cause problems when they spread over into people's farmland and orchards. The people cannot move over to make room for the bears. Instead, they often attack and kill the bears.

The bears' other problem is that people are afraid of them. Brown, polar and black bears are much stronger than humans. Polar bears sometimes hunt people for food, when they can find nothing else to eat. Brown and black bears have also attacked and even killed humans. However, this only happens if a person startles a bear, or comes between a female and her cubs.

Polar bears sometimes look for food on rubbish dumps in the town of Churchill, Canada. People must keep out of their way.

Because people are afraid of bears, they have hunted them for thousands of years. In Europe there are not many brown bears left because so many have been killed. When Europeans went to North America, they killed as many bears as they could. Both Native Americans and the Inuit of Arctic regions kill bears for food and clothing, but they kill only as many bears as they need.

The smaller bears suffer less from hunting nowadays. Today, these bears are in danger because their forest **habitat** is being destroyed.

Above *Black bears like to climb trees. When humans cut down the forests they live in, the bears have nowhere else to go.*

Left *Every year, large areas of tropical forest in Malaysia are burnt and cleared for farmland. Many animals, including sun bears, can only live in this tropical forest.*

BEARS IN DANGER

Brown bear

Brown bears were once quite common in northern countries of the world. However, in Europe these bears are now very **rare** because so many were killed by people in the past. In Scandinavia and eastern Europe all together a few thousand bears survive, but in Spain only about thirty are left.

In Canada, Alaska, and the northern USSR, there are still many brown bears. This is because these countries still have large areas of land without people. North American people call brown bears 'grizzlies'. In the rest of the USA there are 1,000 grizzlies left: in 1800, there were over 100,000 grizzlies.

The grizzly's main problem is that it breeds very slowly. A female might have as many as three cubs at one time.

Brown bear (also called Grizzly bear)

Scientific name: *Ursus arctos* (European brown bear)
Ursus horribilis (Grizzly bear)

Length head to tail: 2.0 – 2.8 m.

Weight: female 80 – 205 kg; male up to 440 kg .

Distribution: Many bears still live in Arctic Canada and Alaska. 1,000 left in rest of USA. Several thousand brown bears survive in USSR and eastern Europe. A few hundred bears left in Norway and Sweden; only about thirty left in Spain.

Habitat: forest and open grasslands.

She must look after them until they are three or even four years old. She only starts a new family when her young can look after themselves. This means that when people started to kill grizzlies in large numbers, not enough new bears were born to replace those that were killed.

There are still some brown bears left in Scandinavian forests. This one was photographed in Sweden.

Grizzly bears are at risk because people are destroying their habitat. In many places, the woods and meadows grizzlies live in have been turned into farmland.

Left *Many North American forests have been cut down for timber or cleared for farmland. Grizzlies like to live in these wild forests.*

In North America many people dislike grizzlies because they raid rubbish dumps and even occasionally kill farmers' calves. The main cause of death for grizzly bears is hunting for sport. People feel very brave if they can kill a grizzly bear because they think it is a frightening animal.

It is not hard to understand why people are afraid of grizzlies. A full-grown bear weighs half a tonne. It is very strong and can charge at 50 kph.

Cruel traps like this were once used to catch and injure bears. Now these traps are against the law.

Bear Country

All Bears Are Dangerous
Bears Enter This Campground
Keep A Clean Camp
Use Extreme Caution

A notice in Yellowstone National Park, USA, warns campers to take care when bears are around.

In Denali National Park, Alaska, bears are protected. Lucky visitors sometimes see grizzlies sleeping in the daytime.

However, people can walk about in bear country without being harmed, if they behave in the right way. In Denali National Park, Alaska, grizzly bears are very common. Everyone who visits Denali is taught what to do when they arrive. If people camp there, they must keep all food in boxes which the bears cannot open. When the visitors walk, they must sing or clap their hands. Some people wear bells which ring as they walk. All these things let the bears know that people are coming. Then the grizzlies are not taken by surprise and alarmed into attacking someone. Although people have come very close to grizzlies in Denali, no one has ever been badly hurt.

American black bear

American black bear

Scientific name: *Ursus americanus*

Length head to tail: 1.3 – 1.8 m.

Weight: female 70 – 120 kg ;
        male up to 270 kg.

Distribution: northern Mexico to Alaska and Great Lakes.

Habitat: woodland and forest.

American black bears are most often killed when hunted for sport, like grizzly bears. However, the black bear is not in as much danger as the grizzly because it can breed more quickly. A female can produce three cubs every two years.

Also, black bears live in woodlands and forests more than in open country, and they have learned to hide from people.

Black bears often climb trees. They need forests to survive.

Black bear cubs are born at the same time as grizzly cubs, in January or February. They are tiny, weighing only about 250 g. Like grizzlies, they stay in the den with their mother, feeding on her milk, until April or May. Then they emerge and travel with their mother until they are about one and a half years old.

A mother black bear feeds her two small cubs on milk. They will stay with her for at least one and a half years.

Park rangers have fitted a radio collar to this sleeping black bear. They will be able to keep track of the bear by following radio signals given out by the collar.

They spend their first winter in their mother's den. Before the second winter comes, they are usually grown up enough to make their own way in the world.

Once many black bears lived as far south as northern Mexico. Today few of them live in Mexico because most of their forest homes have been cut down to make farms and ranches.

Polar bear

Polar bears live in the Arctic. In fact, the Arctic gets its name from 'arctos', the Greek word for a bear. Polar bears are the biggest **carnivorous** land animals in the world. Their home is the open ice and the snow-covered islands around the North Pole.

With their thick fur, polar bears are suited to their cold Arctic home. In the wild, they could not survive anywhere else.

Polar bear

Scientific name: *Ursus maritimus*

Length head to tail: 2 – 3 m.

Weight: female 175 – 300 kg; male up to 650 kg.

Distribution: all around North Pole.

Habitat: sea ice, islands and coasts.

Polar bears are very good swimmers, with thick waterproof fur and a layer of fat to keep them warm. They have skin between their toes, so that their feet are partly webbed. In the Arctic summer, when the ice breaks up, polar bears can swim long distances between the islands of ice.

Polar bears can swim soon after they are born.

Although polar bears mostly hunt seals, sometimes they catch wild ducks.

Polar bears hunt seals across the snow. Their white coat helps to hide them until it is too late for the seal to escape. In winter, the bears move out to the edge of the ice, looking for patches of open water where they can still find seals and sea lions to eat. Male polar bears do not need to make a den in the winter, because they can find seals all the year round.

Inuit have been hunting polar bears with spears for hundreds of years. They eat the meat and use the bear's furry skin to make warm blankets. Polar bears are not in danger from the Inuit hunters because they only kill small numbers. However, when Europeans came to the Arctic, they wanted to sell polar bear skins. They paid the Inuit to kill many bears, and before long polar bears were rare in some parts of the Arctic.

An Inuit man skins a polar bear he has hunted. He is wearing trousers made of polar bear fur.

In the early 1970s wildlife workers decided that too many polar bears were being killed. In 1973 the Arctic countries (USSR, Canada, USA, Greenland and Norway) agreed to hunt fewer bears. Today, no more than a thousand bears are killed each year, mostly by Inuit and other traditional hunters. Now that the bears are better protected, they are no longer in danger.

Polar bears are bred in zoos all over the world but they cannot enjoy life as much as wild polar bears.

Now that they are protected by people, polar bears face a brighter future.

Forest bears

There are four species of forest bears. They all live in the tropics. The sloth bear and the Asian black bear live in parts of India and South-east Asia; the sun bear lives in Malaysia. The spectacled bear lives in South America.

These four forest bear species are all mainly fruit-eaters and so they are a nuisance to people who try to grow crops. Because of this, some of these forest bears were killed by people. Today forest bears are all in danger.

Spectacled bear

Scientific name: *Tremarctos ornatus*

Length head to tail 1.2 – 1.4 m.

Weight: male 130 kg;
female 60 kg.

Distribution: the Andes, from Venezuela to Bolivia and Chile.

Habitat: forested regions from 200 to 4,200 m.

Spectacled bears get their name from the pale rings around their eyes, which look rather like a pair of glasses.

The main danger is that the forests they live in are being cleared to make way for more crop-growing land.

The sloth bear feeds on insects, fruits, flowers and honey. In India people used to be paid to shoot sloth bears because they ate fruit crops.

The spectacled bear lives in South America, high in the mountains. It feeds on fruits and loves the leaf buds of young palm trees. It is hunted for its skin. However, spectacled bears are probably safe in the highest parts of the mountains because people very rarely go there.

Sloth bear

Scientific name: *Melursus ursinus*

Length: head to tail 1.4 – 2.0 m.

Weight: 90 – 115 kg.

Distribution: eastern India and Sri Lanka.

Habitat: forests.

Right *Sloth bears are rarely seen in the wild today. You are more likely to see them in a zoo, as in this photograph.*

Sun bear

Scientific name: *Ursus malayanus*

Length head to tail 1.4 m.

Weight: male 65 kg; female 50 kg.

Distribution: southern China, Burma, Malaysia, Sumatra, Laos, Cambodia, Vietnam, Borneo.

Habitat: Dense parts of tropical rainforests, lowlands and highlands.

The sun bear eats mostly fruits and leaf buds, but also earthworms, small mammals and birds. Its numbers are falling very fast because the Malaysian forests, where it lives, are being destroyed so quickly. Nobody is sure how many of these small forest bears survive. They are difficult to count because they live in such dense forests. There is a danger that people may not realize how rare these bears have become until it is too late to save them.

Sun bears move around at night. This one is looking for food in a tropical forest in Borneo, South-east Asia.

Asian black bear

Scientific name: *Ursus thibetanus*

Length head to tail: 1.3 – 1.7 m.

Weight: up to 120 kg.

Distribution: southern and south-east Asia to western India, Pakistan and Afghanistan; also China, Japan and Korea.

Habitat: forests and shrubby areas in lowland and mountainous regions.

In the past many Asian black bears were used by people as dancing bears. People used to catch a young black bear and thread a rough rope through its nose. When the rope was pulled, the bear would stand up and shake its head because of the pain. Then its owner would collect money from people who watched the bear 'dancing'. Today this cruel practice has almost stopped, but only because these bears have become so rare that people cannot find them.

Many Asian black bears live in mountain forests of Asia. When their forests are cut down, the bears are left homeless.

WHAT GOOD ARE BEARS ?

What would happen if all bears became **extinct**? Adult polar bears eat a seal every day, but if these bears died out, it would not make much difference to the seal **population**. The spare seals would starve if they could not find enough fish to eat. Both grizzly and American black bears feed on salmon in summer. By eating dead and dying fish, the bears help to keep the river banks clean. But if the bears were not there, there would still be plenty of gulls to eat the fish.

Sun bears share their forest home with tropical birds, monkeys and many other unusual animals. They all need the tropical forests to survive.

Grizzly bears help nature by eating dead and dying fish.

The small forest bears eat mostly fruits and leaves. They help to spread the seeds of fruit trees in their droppings. However, plenty of other animals live in these forests. If the small forest bears died out, the forest would go on much as before. Without bears, the natural world would still survive.

However, bears have one very important use for people. Because they need to live in wild, natural places, they can show us how much undamaged land we have left. While there are still some bears, we know that there are still some completely wild areas. If all the bears die out, we shall know that the wild land is running out.

A grizzly bear and her cub explore a wild area of Alaska. Bears need large, open areas like this.

PROTECTING BEARS

The main problem for bears – and for all animals – is that there are too many people in the world. Many places where bears used to live are now cities and farmland. If we want bears to survive, we must set aside places where they can live in safety, such as national parks. These are large areas of protected countryside, where people are not allowed to hunt animals.

Today bear-hunting is banned or carefully controlled in many countries. In Romania, brown bears are protected and their numbers have grown to about 4,000. In France the last brown bear was killed about fifty years ago. Now wildlife experts are hoping to **reintroduce** brown bears into the Alps.

The mother of this black bear cub was killed. Luckily an American wildlife worker saved the cub and looked after it.

If we look after the world's wild places, we can enjoy them and so can bears. This grizzly bear is cleaning its paws in a lovely summer meadow.

An international **organization** called **CITES** strictly controls the buying and selling of skins and other parts of rare animals. CITES protects all bears except the American black bear and the sloth bear, which are not yet in serious danger.

Wherever bears are found, they make a place more wild and exciting. But bears are not just beautiful, exciting animals: they have a right to share our planet with us. If we look after them, bears will be roaming wild forests for many years to come.

Glossary

Breeding season The time of year when male and female bears produce their young.

Carnivorous Meat-eating.

CITES The Convention on the International Trade in Endangered Species. This organization keeps watch on the trade in rare animals.

Cubs Young bears.

Extinct Gone for ever from the Earth.

Habitat The place where an animal lives. A woodland, a lake and a meadow are all different kinds of habitat.

Mate To come together as a male and a female to produce babies.

Organization A group of people who work together.

Population The numbers of a species that live in a certain area.

Reintroduce To put a species of animal back into an area where it onced lived. Humans can bring in animals bred in zoos or wild animals from other areas.

Rare Very few in number.

Species A group of living things which are alike and able to breed with each other.

Territory An area in which an animal lives and breeds. An animal defends its territory against other animals.

Tropics The hot parts of the world near the equator.

Further reading

Bears Norman Barrett (Colour Library, 1988).

Bears in the Wild Cliff Moon (Wayland, 1985).

Bears of the World Domico & Newman (Facts on File, 1988).

Endangered Animals Malcolm Penny (Wayland, 1988).

Polar Bear/Project Wildlife series Michael Bright (Franklin Watts, 1989).

Wildlife in Danger Robert Burton (Macmillan, 1981).

Useful addresses

If you would like to help to protect bears and other rare animals of the world, you may like to join one of the organizations listed below.

Australian Conservation Foundation
672b Glenferrie Road
Hawthorn
Victoria 3122

Environment and Conservation Organizations of New Zealand (ECO)
PO Box 11057
Wellington

Watch club
Royal Society for Nature Conservation
22 The Green
Nettleham
Lincs LN2 2NR
England

Worldwide Fund for Nature (Australia)
Level 17
St Martin's Tower
31 Market Street
GPO BOX 528
Sydney NSW 2001

Worldwide Fund for Nature (Canada)
60 Saint Clair Avenue East
Suite 201
Toronto
Ontario M4T 1N5

Worldwide Fund for Nature (UK)
Panda House
Weyside Park
Catteshall Lane
Godalming
Surrey GU7 1XR

Picture acknowledgements

The publishers would like to thank the following: Bryan and Cherry Alexander 19 below, 20; Frank Lane Picture Agency 24 (Mark Newman); all other photographs from Oxford Scientific Films by the following photographers: Maurice Carlisle 18; John Chellman 22; Margot Conte 21 left; Judd Cooney 11 above, 16; David C Fritts 5 above, 6, 26 below; Philippe Henry 13 above; Frank Huber 15; Richard Kolar 13 below; Michael Leach 14 below; Leonard Lee Rue 10, 27; Zigmund Leszczynski 8, 17 above, 23; Ted Levin 19 above; Joe McDonald 17 below, 28; Stan Osolinski 7 above; Wendy Shattil and Bod Rozinski 5 below, 29; John Stern 26 above; Stouffer Productions Ltd 9 above, 14 above; Charles Tyler 11 below; Tom Ulrich *cover*, 7 below, 9 below, 21 right; Belinda Wright 25. The map on page 4 is by Jenny Hughes.

Index